*SPORT HAS THE POWER
TO CHANGE THE WORLD.*

NELSON MANDELA

About the author:

Phil H. Graff, born in Luxembourg in 1981, has spent over 15 years researching what distinguishes particularly healthy, robust, and long-lived individuals. Focusing on studies published in peer-reviewed scientific medical journals, Phil offers practical advice on how to best feed ourselves and our families to maximize endurance and strength. He studied economics with a focus on health economics and worked in the management of an international food giant before he became a well-known nutrition coach and consultant, author of plant-based nutrition books, and serial entrepreneur.

PHIL H. GRAFF

PLANT
VICTORIOUS

**HOW ATHLETES CAN PUSH THEIR
PERFORMANCE LIMITS WITH PLANTS.**

CONTENTS

*IF YOU WANT SOMETHING
YOU HAVE NEVER HAD,
YOU MUST BE WILLING
TO DO SOMETHING
YOU HAVE NEVER DONE.*

THOMAS JEFFERSON

Introduction

What's the performance difference between a gold and silver medal? A fraction of one percent. That's why many athletes have resorted to performance-enhancing remedies. However, legal medications and dietary supplements have countless risks and side effects that can seriously harm athletes' health. Why do so many professional and recreational athletes nevertheless take these risks when natural foods without any health risks but loads of positive side effects (including protection against diseases) exist? Natural foods have a nice side effect for your wallet too: These untreated nutrients are much cheaper and easier to get (available in virtually every supermarket) than expensive and heavily marketed sports supplements.

Many athletes believe that specially formulated dietary supplements are essential for optimal sports nutrition. However, this widespread opinion is most commonly based upon advertising claims from dietary supplement manufacturers or individual studies performed or paid for by the manufacturer. In this book, we focus on facts based on broad scientific consensus. Independent and peer-reviewed research shows that whole plant-based foods, with their broad spectrum of nutrients and phytochemicals, regularly outperform concentrated or isolated dietary supplements or drugs in terms of improving sports performance or the health of athletes in general.

Nutrient deficiencies and poor eating habits can affect performance. Therefore, before we get to the performance-enhancing and regeneration-accelerating foods, we first address the nutritional foundations that any ambitious athlete, professional or hobbyist, should adhere to in order to maintain optimal long-term fitness levels and good health without unnecessary risks.

As an athlete, you burn calories to perform and thus need to absorb extra energy. That means the energy consumed must be equally compensated for to maintain a constant body weight. Those who consume fewer calories than they burn for intensive exercise risk losing bone density and muscle mass; women also risk menstrual dysfunctions.[1] The ideal athlete's diet is plant-based because it is rich in carbohydrates and low in fat.[2] The best calories come from carbohydrate-rich foods with low fat and adequate protein content.[1] In addition, plant-based nutrition, with its high content of vitamins, minerals, and antioxidants, protects us from the effects of high training loads (including free radicals) and guarantees a perfect energy supply for our muscles.

Let's start with the most important building block of sports nutrition: **carbohydrates**.

Carbohydrates are primarily stored in the muscles and liver. Countless studies show that carbohydrates boost performance and stamina.[3] Carbohydrates are the principal source of energy used during intense workouts. The specific recommendations for competitive athletes range from 6 to 10 g per kg (or 2.7 to 4.5 g/lb) of body weight.[1] Incidentally, this also corresponds to the values for non-competitive athletes, who should get at least 55% of their calories from carbohydrates. The healthiest sources are whole grains, vegetables, and of course fruits. A carbohydrate-rich diet ensures optimal storage of carbohydrates in the body, which provide the body with energy during exercise and keep the performance of both endurance[4] and weight-training athletes[5] at a consistently high level.

The optimum is complex carbohydrates, which supply energy for a long time. These include whole grains in the form of pasta, bread, or rice, which also provide fiber, vitamins, and minerals. Entirely different is the case with simple carbohydrates or sugars, as found in sweets, jams, or soft drinks. They only bring empty calories without any health benefits for the athlete.

Building block no. 2: **protein.**

In comparison to carbohydrates, protein provides lit-tle in energy reserves.[6] The most important function of protein is the preservation, development, and re-pair of body tissue and of course muscle tissue. A colorful mix of grains, legumes, and vegetables pro-vides us with all the essential amino acids. Vegetable proteins are preferable to animal proteins, as they contain fiber, which among other benefits balances blood sugar levels and gets digestion going. Since meat lacks fiber, eating it makes you feel lazy fast and re-sults in constipation. Animal protein is, therefore, a suboptimal source of healthy proteins for optimal performance. For highly active athletes, protein levels of 1.2 to 1.7 g per kg (or 0.5 to 0.8 g/lb) of body weight per day are recommended[1]; for all others, 0.8 g per kg is recommended.[7]

If you want to take in additional protein, then tofu, seitan, or tempeh are well-advised. Concentrated sources of protein are actually unnecessary for ath-letes or anybody else (see the protein requirements above). Legumes, such as chickpeas, black beans, or kidney beans, are excellent sources of protein and do not damage kidney function like concentrated pro-teins do. Too much protein is not only dangerous for the kidneys, but it can cause body fat percentage to rise, calcium to break down, and the risk of dehydration to increase. Not infrequently, a focus on protein intake leads to a low intake of carbohydrates, the most important source of energy during athletic exercise of all kinds.

Topic: **Fat.**

Most scientists do not recommend high-fat diets for competitive athletes. Everyone should avoid animal fats because of their high content of saturated fatty acids. Nuts and seeds provide abundant healthy fats.

Foods with optimal energy balance are the focus of every ambitious athlete. Optimum energy balance nutrition means foods that require as little energy as possible when they are consumed to make their power available to the body. Food that needs a lot of effort (energy) for digestion makes you tired and weak and unable to achieve top performance. Here, the clear winners are fresh fruits and vegetables. Pseudocereals, such as quinoa or buckwheat, follow in second place. These grains provide very easily digestible, high-quality carbohydrates in brilliant composition with proteins.

Without **hydration,** no peak performance.

The need for hydration increases with physical exertion. Optimum fluid supply is crucial to prevent injury and achieve peak performance. Inadequate hydration or dehydration (body water loss of 1% or more) causes symptoms such as fatigue, headache, or even dark colored urine with a strong smell. It leads to heat stroke,[8] neuromuscular fatigue,[9] and convulsions. These consequences and symptoms are avoidable by drinking about a cup (or 250 ml) of water at least 8 times per day. Scientists make the following general recommendations on the amount of fluid that should be ingested in preparation for, during, and after exercise:[10]

-Two hours before exercise: Drink about 2 cups (500 ml) of fluid.
-During exercise: About 0.5 to 1.5 cups (150 to 350 ml) of fluid every 15 to 20 minutes.
-After exercise: About 2 to 3 cups (500 to 700 ml) of fluid for 1 pound (half-kilogram) body weight loss.

Weigh yourself before and after every exercise to determine your fluid loss. You are probably sufficiently hydrated if your urine is pale yellow.

Natural water is the best beverage for activities lasting up to one hour. If activities last longer than 60 to 90 minutes, sports drinks containing carbohydrates or electrolytes can be helpful both during and after exercise.[11]

Top athletes „powered by plants"

More and more world-class athletes decide to go plant-based for reasons of performance optimization and health. Plant-based athletes compete in the NFL, running, tennis, weightlifting, swimming, surfing, boxing, figure skating, triathlons, auto racing, the NBA, cycling, skiing, snowboarding, and more:

Kyrie Irving (five-time NBA All-Star)

Venus Williams (one of the all-time greats of women's tennis)

Lewis Hamilton (one of the greatest F1 drivers of all time)

Carl Lewis ("Sportsman of the Century" voted by the International Olympic Committee)

Dotsie Bausch (eight-time US national cycling champion)

Hannah Teter (Olympic champion, snowboarder)

Morgan Mitchell (two-time Australian 400m champion)

Kendrick Farris (American record-holding weightlifter)

Meagan Duhamel (Olympic champion, pair skater)

Patrik Baboumian (world record-holding strongman)

James Wilks (winner of The Ultimate Fighter)

Seba Johnson (youngest alpine ski racer in Olympic history, vegan from birth)

Brendan Brazier (Ironman triathlete)

Bryant Jennings (boxing heavyweight title contender)

Scott Jurek (record-holding ultra-marathoner)

Tia Blanco (two-time world surfing champion)

Aaron Simpson (record-holding mixed martial artist)

Rip Esselstyn (triathlete and former firefighter)

David Carter (American football defensive end, NFL)

Rich Roll (ultra-endurance athlete)

Cam F. Awesome (US boxing champion)

Fiona Oakes (holds 4 records for marathon running)

Tim Shieff (world-champion freerunner)

Mac Danzig (winner of The Ultimate Fighter)

Leilani Münter (one of the top ten female race car drivers in the world)

Steph Davis (one of the world's leading climbers)

Jermain Defoe (professional Premier League footballer)

David Haye (professional boxer and world champion)

Derrick Morgan (American football linebacker, NFL)

These are some of the most well-known vegan athletes. Other elite athletes are making the switch to plant-based diets.

Scientific Sources:

1. Position of the American Dietetic Association, Dietitians of Canada, and the American College of Sports Medicine: Nutrition and athletic performance. **Journal of the American Dietetic Association** 2009;109:509-527, Rodriguez NR, Dimarco NM, Langley S

2. Vegetarian dietary practices and endurance performance. The **American Journal of Clinical Nutrition** 1988;48(3suppl):754-761, Nieman DC

3. Guidelines for daily carbohydrate intake: do athletes achieve them? **Sports Medicine** 2001;31:267-299, Burke LM, Cox GR, Culmmings NK, Desbrow B

4. Nutritional needs of elite endurance athletes. Part I: carbohydrate and fluid requirements. **European Journal of Sports Science** 2005;5:3-14, Tarnopolsky MA, Gibala M, Jeukendrup AE, et al.

5. Carbohydrate supplementation and resistance training. **The Journal of Strength & Conditioning Research** 2003;17:187-196, Haff GG, Lehmkuhl MJ, McCoy LB, Stone MH

6. Carbohydrate Metabolism and exercise. In: Wolinsky I, Hickson JF, eds. **Nutrition in Exercise and Sport**. 3rd ed. London: CRC Press; 1998, Liebman M, Wilkinson JG

7. **Food and Nutrition Board, Institute of Medicine**: Dietary Reference Intakes for Energy, Carbohydrate, Fiber, Fat, Fatty Acids, Cholesterol, Protein, and Amino Acids (Macronutrients). Washington, DC: National Academy Press; 2005

8. Water: an essential but overlooked nutrient. **Journal of the American Dietetic Association** 1999;99:200-206, Kleiner SM

9. Effect of fluid ingestion on neuromuscular function during prolonged cycling exercise. **British Journal of Sports Medicine** 2005;39:e17, Vallier JM, Grego F, Basset F, Lepers R, Bernard T, Brisswalter J

10. American College of Sports Medicine position stand. Exercise and fluid replacement. **Medicine & Science in Sports & Exercise** 2007;39:377, Sawka MN, Burke LM, Eichner ER, et al.

11. Nutrient beverages for exercise and sport. In: Wolinsky I, Hickson JF, eds. **Nutrition in Exercise and Sport.** 3rd ed. London: CRC Press; 1998, Puhl SM, Buskirk ER

I'VE MISSED MORE THAN 9000 SHOTS IN MY CAREER. I'VE LOST ALMOST 300 GAMES. 26 TIMES, I'VE BEEN TRUSTED TO TAKE THE GAME WINNING SHOT AND MISSED. I'VE FAILED OVER AND OVER AND OVER AGAIN IN MY LIFE. AND THAT IS WHY I SUCCEED.

MICHAEL JORDAN

Performance Enhancement – Before Sports

Beetroot
- Effective, Natural Doping

Well-toned muscles and an optimal supply of oxygen to these muscles are the basis of sporting excellence. The energy we can draw from oxygen always stays the same—that's what I believed until I learned of the incredible powers beetroot can release.

Some studies on professional athletes show promising outcomes. For example, racing cyclists improved their results on a 16-kilometer (about 10 miles) route by 45 seconds on average after drinking beetroot juice. During intensive training, the advantage of beetroot becomes obvious. Here, the cyclists were able to extend their time to exhaustion by a full 1 min 32 sec. The cyclists consumed 19% less oxygen and achieved better endurance. In other words, beetroot juice optimizes energy production in the human body. No medications (legal or illegal) or dietary supplements can match up to plain beetroot juice.[1]

Every professional and recreational athlete reading this will now want to know the right "dosage" to maximize performance. Approximately three cooked beetroots[2] or half a cup (120 ml) of beetroot juice are the ideal amounts. The optimal timing is between 2 and 3 hours before the start of the competition.[3]

In addition to its performance-enhancing potential in sports, beetroot is also effective against hypertension. On average, blood pressure can be lowered by 8 points with approximately one cup (240 ml) of beetroot juice per day, with better results if taken regularly.[4] Those who take antihypertensive medications should consult their doctor. The effect of beetroot should not be underestimated. The main advantage of a natural plant solution over medicines is freedom from unpleasant side effects, not to mention minimized healthcare costs.

Another positive side effect of beetroot: Not only are the muscles better supplied with oxygen, but so is the brain. This significantly slows the progression of dementia in the elderly. With age, the blood supply to particular regions of the brain deteriorates and leads to a decrease in perceptiveness and even dementia. Drinking beetroot juice can improve the flow of blood and oxygen to critical brain regions.[5]

Fenugreek
and Strength Training

What beetroot and other nitrate-containing vegetables offer for endurance, fenugreek offers for weight training. Fenugreek has a tremendously positive influence on the development of strength in the lower and upper body. In one experiment, participants who ate powdered fenugreek (500 mg) achieved up to 40 kg (88 lbs) extra in the leg press.[6] The study was undertaken with the highest standards, including a double-blind trial. No side effects were detected.

Fenugreek not only improves muscle strength but seems to hold promise in the fight against cancer cells. Fenugreek effectively fights prostate cancer cells and other cancer cells. In contrast to conventional cancer medications, the spice does not attack healthy cells.[7] Not only can stronger muscles be achieved without side effects, which is already remarkable, but you also get complementary protection against cancer cells. One of the forefathers of the naturopathic medicine movement, Sebastian Kneipp, already knew this outstanding effect: "Fenugreek is the best of all remedies for dissolving tumors and ulcers that I know of."

Ground fenugreek (seeds) is a tasty and exotic spice (spicy-salty, markedly bitter). It is an integral part of curry powder and goes particularly well with vegetarian dishes, such as lentils, spinach, or potatoes. It is a common ingredient in Asian and African bread. Many Indian meals use fenugreek by default.

If you do not like the taste of fenugreek spices, then you can place them in empty capsules. Unlike dietary supplements, you know for sure what's inside and the homemade capsules are, of course, much cheaper.

Peppermint Power

Mint, probably one of the most commonly used herbs, has known analgesic, antispasmodic, and antioxidant effects. But mint can do even more: It can improve sports performance. About two cups (0.5 liter) of water supplemented with a small drop (0.05 ml) of peppermint oil can enhance performance by over 20%.[8] Participants consumed two cups (half a liter) daily of the aforementioned mixture for 10 days to obtain these results.

Alternatively, a fresh-tasting variant is possible as mint water: Put just a few peppermint leaves in two cups (half a liter) of water in the refrigerator overnight. Or even healthier: Mix fresh peppermint leaves with water in a blender to get a little green at the same time. A peppermint plant can be grown effortlessly in the kitchen for a constant fresh supply of mint leaves. Mint is fun to add to many recipes, whether breakfast, lunch, or dessert.

For some athletes, the smell of peppermint alone is motivating. Therefore, if you do not like the taste of peppermint, you can try inhaling mint oil.

THE BEST FRUIT
AGAINST MUSCLE SORENESS

Muscle soreness develops in the days after an extreme physical effort. The pain is due to inflammation caused by small micro-cracks in the muscles.

In a study, the participants' biceps were deliberately overloaded by having them raise extreme weights again and again. The next day, all subjects suffered from severe pain and a 22% loss of strength in their arms. Now, one group had been given one and a half cups (355 ml) of cherry juice twice a day starting 4 days before the training. This group had significantly less pain after overwork and a power loss of just 4% the following day.[9]

For marathon runners, cherry juice has been shown to reduce the recovery phase significantly, and runners' muscle pain was markedly lower than in a control group.[10] Speeding up the recovery phase is unquestionably one of the most important goals for coaches of every sport.

Cherry juice was used in these studies because a control group could just drink a cherry-flavored red beverage. Presumably, fresh cherries are at least as effective as the juice and are even healthier because of their fiber and other natural phytonutrients.

If you don't have cherries or cherry juice on hand, try berries. Blueberries are impressively effective against muscle soreness. Consuming 9 oz (250 g) of blueberries regularly (every day) and enjoying an additional 13 oz (375 g) of berries 1 to 2.5 h before extreme sports reduces oxidative stress and inflammation and strengthens the immune system.[11]

Watermelon is another effective and tasty fruit. Two cups (500 ml) of mixed watermelons before strenuous training reduce inflammation and thus muscle soreness[12] while simultaneously providing a delicious drink before training.

With pure and delicious cherries, berries, and watermelons, you can realize results that would otherwise be achievable only with medications with not inconsiderable risks and side effects. And as it turns out, you do not have to eat the same thing every day, but you can achieve similar results with different and tasty kinds of fruit.

MUSIC AS LEGAL DOPING

Listening to music during the warm-up before short-term, high-intensity physical effort improves sporting results.[13] Listening for 10 minutes to music with a very fast tempo (>120-140 beats per minute) enhances performance. This effect is measurable both in terms of peak performance (p peak) and average performance (p mean).[13] The great thing is that the whole procedure is completely legal in top-level sports and unquestionably, absolutely free of side effects.

By the way, music, as most people know, is also a good source of motivation in everyday training. Here, the lyrics (like the repetitive affirmation "We are the champions..." and similar positive verses) are for many athletes more effective than a high frequency. For performance-enhancing music just before the competition, a very fast tempo is essential.

More information about sports and music is found in the chapter Achievement Motivation: Motivation over the Ears.

Scientific Sources of the Chapter Performance Enhancement – Before Sports:

1. Dietary nitrate supplementation reduces the O2 cost of low-intensity exercise and enhances tolerance to high-intensity exercise in humans. **Journal of Applied Physiology** 2009;107(4):1144-1155, Bailey S., Winyard P., Vanhatalo A., Blackwell J., et al.

2. Vascular effects of dietary nitrate (as found in green leafy vegetables and beetroot) via the nitrate-nitrite-nitric oxide pathway. **British Journal of Clinical Pharmacology** 2013;75(3):677-696, Lidder S., Webb A.

3. Beetroot juice and exercise: pharmacodynamic and dose-response relationships. **Journal of Applied Physiology** 2013;115(3):325-336, Wylie L., Kelly J., Bailey S., Blackwell J., et al.

4. Dietary nitrate provides sustained blood pressure lowering in hypertensive patients: a randomized, phase 2, double-blind, placebo controlled study. **Hypertension** 2015;65(2):320-327, Kapil V., Khambata R., Robertson A., et al.

5. Acute effect of a high nitrate diet on brain perfusion in older adults. **Nitric oxide** 2011;24(1):34-42, Presley T., Morgan A., Bechthold E., Clodfelter W., Dove R., et al.

6. The effects of a commercially available botanical supplement on strength, body composition, power output, and hormonal profiles in resistance-trained males. **Journal of the international society of sports nutrition** 2010 Oct 27;7:34, Poole C, Bushey B, Foster C, Campbell B, Willoughby D, Kreider R, Taylor L, Wilborn C

7. Fenugreek: a naturally occurring edible spice as an anti-cancer agent. **Cancer biology and therapy** 2009

Feb;8(3):272-8, Shabbeer S, Sobolewski M, Anchoori RK, Kachhap S, Hidalgo M, Jimeno A, Davidson N, Carducci MA, Khan SR

8. The effects of peppermint on exercise performance **Journal of the International Society of Sports Nutrition** 2013; 10: 15 Abbas Meamarbashi, Ali Rajabi

9. Efficacy of a tart cherry juice blend in preventing the symptoms of muscle damage. **British journal of sports medicine** 2006 Aug;40(8):679-83, Connolly DA, McHugh MP, Padilla-Zakour OI, Carlson L, Sayers SP

10. Influence of tart cherry juice on indices of recovery following marathon running. **Scandinavian journal of medicine & science in sports** 2010 Dec;20(6):843-52, Howatson G, McHugh MP, Hill JA, Brouner J, Jewell AP, van Someren KA, Shave RE, Howatson SA

11. Effect of blueberry ingestion on natural killer cell counts, oxidative stress, and inflammation prior to and after 2.5 h of running. **Applied physiology, nutrition and metabolism** 2011 Dec;36(6):976-84, McAnulty LS, Nieman DC, Dumke CL, Shooter LA, Henson DA, Utter AC, Milne G, McAnulty SR

12. Watermelon juice: potential functional drink for sore muscle relief in athletes. **Journal of agricultural and food chemistry** 2013 Aug 7;61(31):7522-8, Tarazona-Díaz MP, Alacid F, Carrasco M, Martínez I, Aguayo E

13. The Effects of Music on High-intensity Short-term Exercise in Well Trained Athletes. **Asian Journal of Sports Medicine** 2012 Dec; 3(4): 233-238 Mohamed Jarraya, PhD, Hamdi Chtourou, PhD, Asma Aloui, PhD, Omar Hammouda, PhD, Karim Chamari, PhD, Anis Chaouachi, PhD, and Nizar Souissi, PhD

I HATED EVERY MINUTE OF TRAINING, BUT I SAID: DON'T QUIT. SUFFER NOW AND LIVE THE REST OF YOUR LIFE AS A CHAMPION.

MUHAMMAD ALI

Performance Retention
– During Sports

RAISINS INSTEAD OF EXPENSIVE ENERGY GELS

Sun-dried raisins are nutrient-rich, handy, tasty, and a low-cost source of concentrated carbohydrates. They can easily compete with many commercially available energy gels, regardless of training load.[1,2]

Raisins have been extensively studied compared to energy gels. But common sense suggests that dried dates or figs may offer similar outcomes. The great thing about dates is that there are so many delicious kinds that everyone can find his favorite variety. In addition, date sugar (dried and ground dates) blends easily with other foods and gives them a mild and pleasant sweetness. Other dried fruits, such as pineapples, papayas, and mangoes, provide fast, super-tasty, and healthy energy.

In contrast to sports gels and similar convenience products, if you eat raisins, dates, and the like, you know exactly what you are getting and avoid the undesirable side effects of the numerous additives and preservatives in industrially made energy gels.

EFFECTIVE PREVENTION OF MUSCLE FATIGUE

If, during strenuous exercise, more lactic acid accumulates in the muscles than can be transported away, a burning pain occurs and we cannot continue exercising. The intake of citrus fruits during sports effectively delays this phenomenon. In one study, two glasses of orange juice significantly delayed muscle fatigue.[3] Since orange juice does not contain fiber, it is best to eat whole oranges instead to keep blood sugar levels down.

Other citrus fruits, whether lemons, limes, or tangerines, are similarly helpful because of their comparable composition. Preparing a box with peeled orange or tangerine slices beforehand makes them easy to access during sports. Citrus fruits last longer and reduce free radicals during training because of their high antioxidant content.

Citrus fruits, like oranges, have a naturally high water content, making them ideal snacks for any sport where adequate hydration is essential.

Nitrate Power
for Being On the Go

The natural nitrates in beetroot are responsible for its performance-enhancing effects. In addition to beetroots, the following vegetables have remarkably high nitrate levels: arugula, rhubarb, cilantro, butter leaf lettuce, basil, beet greens, and chard.[4] However, these products are not practical for a marathon or a long mountain hike, as they are easily perishable and difficult to transport.

Fennel seeds are the solution. They have high nitrate levels[4] and some practical benefits: They weigh virtually nothing, are long-lasting, and can be bought anywhere at competitive prices. Even a small pocket in running pants can transport fennel seeds without problems. In addition, the seeds taste fresh. Chewing dried fennel seeds opens up blood vessels[5] and thus leads to better performances. For mountain climbers at altitudes above 8.200 ft (2.500 m), fennel seeds are interesting not only for their minimal weight and ability to improve the supply of oxygen in the blood, but also because of their preventive effect against the dreaded high-altitude pulmonary edema.[5]

Bananas
vs. Sports Drinks

Endurance and amateur athletes have relied on bananas as an energy source for a long time. An average banana with easily digestible sugars and natural electrolytes provides a whopping 100 calories. Bananas are rich in potassium and other nutrients and are easy to transport for runners, cyclists, and hikers. But that's probably known to most readers. More interesting is the following question: Which is more efficient, a natural banana or a synthetic sports drink?

Let's look at an insightful study where trained cyclists completed a 46-mile (75 km) road race. Half the participants received about one cup (250 ml) of a carbohydrate drink every 15 minutes; the other half got a simple banana with the same timing. The performance of the participants was the same regardless of what they consumed. But a blood test showed the differences: The banana eaters had healthier blood values since they got not only a better sugar mixture from the natural fruit, but natural dietary fiber, potassium, vitamin B6, and of course, antioxidants.[6]

Scientific Sources of the Chapter Performance Retention – During Sports:

1. Sun-dried raisins are a cost-effective alternative to Sports Jelly Beans in prolonged cycling. **The Journal of Strength & Conditioning Research** 2011 Nov;25(11):3150-6 Rietschier HL, Henagan TM, Earnest CP, Baker BL, Cortez CC, Stewart LK

2. Metabolic and performance effects of raisins versus sports gel as pre-exercise feedings in cyclists. **The Journal of Strength & Conditioning Research** 2007 Nov;21(4):1204-7 Kern M, Heslin CJ, Rezende RS

3. Orange juice improved lipid profile and blood lactate of overweight middle-aged women subjected to aerobic training. **Maturitas** 2010 Dec;67(4):343-7, Aptekmann NP, Cesar TB

4. Food sources of nitrates and nitrites: the physiologic context for potential health benefits. **The American journal of clinical nutrition** 2009 Jul;90(1):1-10, Hord NG, Tang Y, Bryan NS

5. Nitrites derived from Foneiculum vulgare (fennel) seeds promotes vascular functions. **Journal of food science** 2012 Dec;77(12):H273-9, Swaminathan A, Sridhara SR, Sinha S, Nagarajan S, Balaguru UM, Siamwala JH, Rajendran S, Saran U, Chatterjee S

6. Bananas as an Energy Source during Exercise: A Metabolomics Approach. **PLoS ONE**, 2012; 7 (5): e37479, David C. Nieman, Nicholas D. Gillitt, Dru A. Henson, Wei Sha, R. Andrew Shanely, Amy M. Knab, Lynn Cialdella-Kam, Fuxia Jin

Performance Acceleration (Reduced Recovery Time) – After Sports

INTRODUCTION

It's a fact that sport is excellent for your health. But how is it that after extreme physical stress (for example, marathons or bicycle races like the Tour de France) so many free radicals are generated that the DNA of some cells can be damaged? At first, this seems contradictory: Sports should be healthy, yet free radicals attack the cell structures of our body. However, the answer is simple: Physical activity itself is not necessarily the healthy part, but rather the regeneration phase after exercise. According to the slogan "what doesn't kill us makes us stronger," sports thus strengthens our defenses against free radicals in the long term.

Scientific studies have investigated the degree of DNA damage before, immediately after, and a week after physical effort. One week after sports, the level of DNA damage was significantly lower than before exercise. Physical stress seems like a vaccine against DNA damage: First, you get a little weaker, and later you are all the stronger.

Natural Inflammation Relief After Workouts

Post-workout inflammation is our bodies' natural reaction to stress. Physical exertion is stress, albeit positive for the body in the long term, because it partially destroys muscle tissue to rebuild even stronger tissue. Increased inflammation is no joke because chronic inflammation can lead to severe diseases. Nevertheless, you want to train again as quickly as possible to achieve new top performances. Natural anti-inflammatory foods alleviate inflammations and shorten the recovery phase, allowing training to be resumed faster. A selection of the most effective foods in the fight against inflammation is presented in this chapter. These foods are not only simple to integrate into any diet but also—depending on individual tastes —can be very delicious.

Dark Green Leafy Vegetables

Dark green leafy vegetables contain concentrated amounts of high-potency antioxidants, vitamins (including C and E), carotenoids, and flavonoids. Every single component listed above already has anti-inflammatory effects, all together are a superweapon against inflammation of all kinds.

Whether kale, spinach, Swiss chard, rocket, or green salads, everyone can find something green that satisfies their own palates. Tasty salad dressings often work wonders. My favorite salad dressing: Put about 3-4 tablespoons almonds, 2-3 tablespoons lemon juice, 2 tablespoons mustard, 1 tablespoon nutritional yeast flakes, 2 tablespoons soy sauce, 1-3 cloves of garlic, and about a half cup of water in a blender and blend until creamy. If you do not have a powerful blender, just take almond butter and mix it with the other ingredients instead of raw almonds.

Turmeric

By adding a pinch of turmeric to our daily diet, the damage caused to DNA by free radicals can be reduced by as much as 50% after one week.[1] Free radicals result from intensive training, and turmeric is one of the most effective methods for combating them. Turmeric contains powerful antioxidants such as glutathione, alpha-lipoic acid, and coenzyme Q10, which can proactively enhance inflammatory processes.

How to integrate this vigorous spice into our everyday lives? Turmeric goes well with all rice dishes, most vegetable soups, and many vegetable meals. Within an hour of being ingested, curcumin (an active ingredient of turmeric) can be detected in the bloodstream, but only in small amounts, as the liver tries to filter out the dye. Here, ordinary black pepper comes into play: Black pepper is about 5% piperine, which prevents the liver from making curcumin water-soluble, and so curcumin cannot be excreted through urine. As a result, the curcumin level in the blood can be increased 20-fold when you eat black pepper and turmeric at the same time![2] So it makes sense to add turmeric, always mixed with pepper, to any food (vegetables, rice, or soups). Ingeniously, one of the main ingredients of curry, in addition to turmeric, is black pepper. And who doesn't like curry dishes?

Garlic

The world's most widely used flavoring is assuredly garlic. The stinking rose, another name for garlic, is rich in anti-inflammatory ingredients such as diallyl disulfide and thiacremonone.[3] Contained substances such as phosphorus, zinc, selenium, arginine, polyphenols, and vitamins B6 and C optimize blood circulation and help prevent inflammation.

Mediterranean and Asian cuisine offer many tasty garlic recipes. A little garlic goes well with almost every vegetable, and sliced fresh garlic can be an aromatic enhancement to salad dressing.

Berries

Berries play in the first league of healthy fruit. Why? They are vividly colored. The anthocyanins (plant dyes) that trigger this rich coloration (for example, the intense blue of fresh blueberries) contain the antioxidants that protect us from free radicals.

Delicious berries (whether fresh or frozen) can be integrated smoothly into a daily routine, whether prepared for breakfast in cereal, in the blender as a smoothie, as a fruity dessert (for example, frozen bananas with frozen strawberries blended to creamy ice), or as a healthy snack in between. Try different berries. You will surely find your favorite variety quickly: raspberries, strawberries, blueberries, goji berries, cranberries, blackberries, acai berries, etc. The more sumptuous the red/black/blue of the berries, the more valuable antioxidants. On an average, berries contain 10-times the antioxidant capacity of other fruits and vegetables.[4]

For athletes, the consumption of goji berries makes sense in particular. These pleasantly sweet berries are a rich source of antioxidants, especially zeaxanthin. This substance promotes optimal eye health,[5] which is necessary for good performance in ball and endurance sports.

Flaxseed

Flaxseed supplies healthy and high-quality omega-3 fatty acids. Increasing omega-3 intake can help reduce inflammation in the body.[6] In addition, flaxseed has only positive side effects, such as protection against breast and prostate cancer, successful treatment of constipation, and even positive results in regulating blood glucose levels.[7]

Crucial to eating flaxseed is to buy them ground or to ground them yourself with a flour mill, coffee grinder, or powerful blender. Otherwise, they will come out of your digestive system the way they came in and cannot give their power to you. How do you integrate flaxseed into your food? Just mix a tablespoon of ground flaxseed into your breakfast cereal. They can also be mixed well into shakes and smoothies for a nutty taste.

Ground flaxseed is much more effective than the flaxseed oil. The seeds are incredible nutrition powerhouses, and these nutrients disappear when you use just the oil. These great seeds are not only an abundant source of lignans but also offer valuable substances like iron, zinc, copper, calcium, protein, potassium, magnesium, folate, and fiber. Even boron, a trace mineral essential for optimum bone health, is included.

Optimal Food
Immediately After Exercise

Post-exercise food intake is crucial for recovery time and the effectiveness of future workouts. The timing is as important as the type of food.

The first 20 to 30 minutes immediately after exercise is the best time to replenish the muscles' glycogen stores and fill up with fluid to counteract the early stages of inflammation. A 4 to 1 carbohydrate to protein ratio, taken immediately after exercise, is an optimal way to replenish muscle glycogen stores.[8] High antioxidant food is the best way to keep inflammation at bay.

Now, which natural food provides a 4 to 1 ratio of carbohydrates to proteins? On the go, you can ideally fall back on a trail mix with a high dry fruit content relative to the nuts. A self-made product with the preferred fruit and nut varieties is not only cheaper but also a delicious alternative to finished products. Those who eat at home can also enjoy a tasty 4 to 1 ratio with a slice of whole-grain bread coated with one tablespoon of nut butter. Nuts are highly suitable because they contain protein, healthy fats, and lots of antioxidants, which fight free radicals.

The second time window is 45 to 90 minutes after training. After replenishing its glycogen store, our body focuses on repairing and building muscle tissue. Now, high-quality protein sources are needed for an optimal recovery phase.

Healthy protein sources include beans and lentils. Legumes are among the healthiest foods in the world. They are an excellent source of high-quality protein, iron, and zinc, contain hardly any saturated fatty acids, are low in sodium and cholesterol-free, and provide plenty of healthy fiber and folic acids.

Quinoa is also an excellent source of complete protein. Quinoa is gluten-free, can be prepared in 15 minutes, and contains 9 g of protein per cup.

Natural sources of antioxidants, such as fresh fruits and vegetables, are necessary to control inflammation. In a green smoothie, you can effortlessly eat delicious fruits and vegetables in concentrated form. Green vegetables especially contain lots of minerals and vitamins alongside high-quality protein.

Strengthening the Immune System After Exhaustion

Marathon runners are at 2 to 6 times more likely to develop symptoms of upper respiratory tract infections after a strenuous marathon or ultramarathon.[9] Professional soccer players also suffer from significantly less immunoglobulin A production (a vital defense barrier against pathogens) during longer competitions (e.g., world championships) and are therefore also exposed to an increased risk of infections.[10] Tennis players (for example, at WTA/ATP tournaments) face the same risk.

A study found that daily intake of the green algae chlorella 4 weeks before a tournament could maintain the function of the immune system, as shown by the excretion of immunoglobulin A in the participants' saliva.[11]

Chlorella blends well into green smoothies or, as the taste is not for everyone, it can be taken in tablet form with meals. It's better to fill empty capsules with chlorella powder instead of buying overpriced dietary supplements.

Certain dietary fibers, which are found in nutritional yeast and brewer's yeast, protect athletes from a weakened immune system after overexertion. The yeast enhances the production of immune cells. A ¾ teaspoon of nutritional yeast after exercise is enough.[12] In a study, marathon runners achieved astonishing health benefits with about one tablespoon of nutritional yeast per day: The risk of an illness after a marathon fell up to 50% compared with other runners. In addition, the runners felt less tired and less tense and even had an increased drive.[13] For future successes, this is important because runners often suffer from a lack of energy and motivation after a marathon.

Nutritional yeast integrates readily into daily food intake as a spicy ingredient in vegetables, sauces, noodles, or rice (you can use less salt). It has a cheese-like taste and is therefore often used by vegans as a cheese substitute.

Scientific Sources of the Chapter Performance Acceleration – After Sports:

1. Bioavailability of herbs and spices in humans as determined by ex vivo inflammatory suppression and DNA strand breaks. **The Journal of the American College of Nutrition** 2012;31(4):288-294, Percival S., Vanden Heuvel J., Nieves C. Montero C., Migliaccio A., Meadors J.

2. Influence of piperine on the pharmacokinetics of curcumin in animals and human volunteers. **Planta Medica** 1998;64(4):353-356, Shoba G., Joy D., Joseph T., Majeed M., Rajendran R., Srinivas P.

3. Anti-inflammatory and arthritic effects of thiacremonone, a novel sulfur compound isolated from garlic via inhibition of NF-kappaB. **Arthritis Research and Therapy** 2009 11(5):R145, Ban JO, et al.

4. The total antioxidant content of more than 3100 foods, beverages, spices, herbs and supplements used worldwide. **Nutrition Journal** 2010;9:3, Carlsen M., Halvorsen B., Holte K., et al.

5. A double-blind, placebo-controlled study on the effects of lutein and zeaxanthin on photostress recovery, glare disability, and chromatic contrast. **Investigative Ophthalmology and Visual Science** 2014 55(12):8583-9, Hammond BR, Fletcher LM, Roos F, Wittwer J, Schalch W

6. The Effects of Diet on Inflammation. **Journal of the American College of Cardiology** 2006 48 (4), Giugliano D, Ceriello A, and Esposito K

7. Flax and flaxseed oil: an ancient medicine & modern functional food. **Journal of Food Science and Technology** 2014;51(9):1633-1653, Goyal A., Sharma V., Upadhyay N., Gill S., Sihag M.

8. International Society of Sports Nutrition position stand: Nutrient Timing. **Journal of the International Society of Sports Nutrition** 2008 5:17, Kerksick et al.

9. Position statement. Part one: Immune function and exercise. **Exercise immunology review** 2011;17:6-63 Walsh NP, Gleeson M, Shephard RJ, Gleeson M, Woods JA, Bishop NC, Fleshner M, Green C, Pedersen BK, Hoffman-Goetz L, Rogers CJ, Northoff H, Abbasi A, Simon P.

10. Salivary IgA as a risk factor for upper respiratory infections in elite professional athletes. **Medicine and science in sports and exercise** 2008 Jul;40(7):1228-36 Neville V, Gleeson M, Folland JP

11. Chlorella intake attenuates reduced salivary SIgA secretion in kendo training camp participants. **Nutrition Journal** 2012 11:103 Otsuki T, Shimizu K, Iemitsu M, Kono I

12. Baker's yeast β-glucan supplementation increases monocytes and cytokines post-exercise: implications for infection risk? **The British journal of nutrition** 2013 Feb 14;109(3):478-86 Carpenter KC, Breslin WL, Davidson T, Adams A, McFarlin BK

13. Effect of BETA 1, 3/1, 6 GLUCAN on Upper Respiratory Tract Infection Symptoms and Mood State in Marathon Athletes. **Journal of sports science & medicine** 2009 Dec 1;8(4):509-15 Talbott S, Talbott J

*CHAMPIONS KEEP PLAYING
UNTIL THEY GET IT RIGHT.*

BILLIE JEAN KING

ACHIEVEMENT MOTIVATION

Motivation
Through the Stomach

More and more studies show a definite link between eating fruits and vegetables and a happier, healthier life regardless of other factors, such as income, illness, or education. But how does this work?

Most fruits and vegetables contain abundant vitamin C, which plays an essential role in the production of dopamine, the "joy of life" neurotransmitter. In addition, their high antioxidant content reduces inflammation of all kinds, which of course increases overall well-being.[1] In studies, the effect of fresh fruits and vegetables was so strong that participants felt energetic on the same day and their mood was measurably better on the following day than ever before.[2]

Competitive athletes are especially under continual pressure to perform. In the long term, this can lead to fatigue due to depressive feelings. Here, instead of resorting to medicines with adverse side effects, daily intake of fruits and vegetables can effectively prevent mood swings.

With a plant-based diet, it is thus possible to increase general well-being and therefore motivation.

Plants contain substances that can increase the amount of serotonin in the brain. Serotonin is sometimes called the happy chemical, because it contributes to happiness and well-being. Which fruits and vegetables deliver the most benefit? The most beneficial varieties are, among others, pineapples, bananas, kiwis, plums, and tomatoes. Interestingly, however, quantity is not as critical as the combination of active ingredients (including the synergy with proteins, for example). In this case, pure seeds seem to work even better. These include sesame seeds, sunflower seeds, and pumpkin seeds.

In order to fully exploit the benefits of fruits, vegetables, and seeds, foods containing arachidonic acid are a no-go, as this acid has a considerable adverse effect on mood. Animal products such as chicken, eggs, beef, fish, pork, and other meat-based products contain this dangerous acid.[3]

MOTIVATION
OVER THE EARS

The right music is not only motivating but performance enhancing. Researchers recommend six criteria for choosing the best music for motivation:

1) an intense, propulsive beat
2) positive lyrics with appropriate associations for each training
3) a rhythm that matches the preferred speed of the exercises
4) melodies that build up
5) themes of sports, training, success, or victory
6) the athlete's own taste in music

For endurance sports, it is advantageous to choose a song with a consistent tempo. Otherwise, you could quickly leave your optimal pace.

The scientific results of music as a motivator are tremendous: Music reduces the subjective perception of low to moderate physical exertion by about 10%.[4] Matching music arouses positive emotions and thus increases enjoyment in daily training.

For beginners and professional athletes alike, music effectively distracts from the exhaustion, fatigue, or even pain that can arise during physical exertion. This applies primarily to endurance sports such as running, cycling, or swimming. Some athletes listen to their preferred music in order to concentrate fully before a competition.

Several studies have observed a connection between music and self-motivation triggered by positive emotions. Thus, challenging training can become much more manageable.[4] But professional athletes are not the only ones who can benefit from music. In rehabilitation, physiotherapy, and the treatment of chronic pain, music can help exhausting exercises feel more effortless and increase the chance of long-term success.

Scientific Sources of the Chapter Achievement Motivation:

1. On carrots and curiosity: eating fruit and vegetables is as-sociated with greater flourishing in daily life. **British journal of health psychology** 2015 May;20(2):413-27, Conner TS, Brookie KL, Richardson AC, Polak MA

2. Many apples a day keep the blues away--daily experiences of negative and positive affect and food consumption in young adults. **British journal of health psychology** 2013 Nov;18(4):782-98, White BA, Horwath CC, Conner TS

3. Vegetarian diets are associated with healthy mood states: a cross-sectional study in seventh day adventist adults. **Nutrition Journal** 2010 Jun 1;9:26, Beezhold BL, Johnston CS, Daigle DR.

4. Music in the exercise domain: a review and synthesis (Part I) **International Review of Sport and Exercise Psychology** 2012 Mar; 5(1): 44–66, Costas I. Karageorghis and David-Lee Priest

Superfoods for Athletes

Superfoods with Potential

Why only potential? Because significant independent studies—as with the foods in the previous chapters—are not yet available for the superfoods in this chapter. But there is potential, as more and more successful athletes attribute a subjective increase in performance to these foods. Some of these superfoods are exorbitantly expensive, so everyone has to decide for themselves whether to invest so much for a possible performance improvement or whether to rely on widely researched and reliable food like beetroot, fenugreek, or cherries instead. Nevertheless, let us discuss some promising superfoods for sports. It is best to test individual foods and to use or to omit them on the basis of your own experience.

Maca Root

Endurance athletes (including marathon runners) especially swear by this medicinal plant. Maca has been cultivated in the Peruvian Andes at altitudes between 9,000 and 11,500 ft for about 2,000 years. Both physical performance and mental capacity are supposed to increase with maca. According to various reports from maca consumers, maca leads to a strengthened immune system, increased sexual desire, and less chronic fatigue and depression. Some marketers are even promoting this root as a natural potency remedy.

In North America and Europe, maca is only available as maca powder. Some athletes mix about 1 tablespoon of maca powder into their daily smoothies.

<u>Fact:</u> The maca root is rich in essential amino acids, vitamins, and minerals. Individual studies, primarily from South America, have gradually confirmed the root's effectiveness.

Chia Seeds

These seeds from Central America are currently experiencing a real hype among the so-called superfoods. For the Aztecs, chia seeds were a staple food. Chia is often referred to as the ultimate runner's food. Nowadays, the distributors in North America and Europe promote chia seeds with considerable marketing efforts.

Chia fans and individual studies attribute longer stamina while exercising, better oxygen intake, and even better heart health to the little seeds. The most common experience reported with chia seeds is a consistent energy supply over a prolonged period. Therefore, there is an increased awareness of chia in the athletic community.

Chia seeds soaked in plant-based milk or water can be used to make a pudding-like substance. Combined with fresh fruit, vanilla, or cinnamon, it can create a delicious plant-based pudding. In smoothies, chia seeds can be used to create a thicker consistency.

Fact: Chia seeds contain omega-3 fatty acids, fiber, antioxidants, and phytonutrients. In nutrient content and effectiveness, they are comparable to flaxseed. But a difference remains: Flaxseed has been researched over hundreds of years and proven to be highly effective for our health.

Spirulina

Dried spirulina, a type of blue-green algae, is said to contain the highest proportion of protein in relation to its weight. It is, of course, more convenient and perhaps safer (and cheaper) to regularly eat a wide range of green plants (kale, spinach, broccoli, etc.) to receive all the essential amino acids.

Studies show a potential link between spirulina consumption, improved endurance, and an accelerated recovery period. You can eat this promising algae as an addition to smoothies.

Fact: Dried spirulina contains all the essential amino acids, beta-carotene, B-vitamins, vitamin A, and plenty of calcium, iron, and magnesium. In order to avoid contamination with poisonous algae, it is crucial to use products that have been cultivated in separate tanks rather than in open lakes. Chlorella is a scientifically sound and safer alternative to spirulina (see the chapter "Strengthening the Immune System After Exhaustion").

Hemp Seeds

Yes, hemp is a variant of the cannabis plant, and no, hemp seeds do not make you "high" or include any harmful substances. On the contrary, hemp seeds are remarkably nutritious. They contain omega-3 fatty acids, omega-6 fatty acids, antioxidants, vitamins (A, B, C, D, and E), and minerals (including magnesium, calcium, potassium, and iron).

For competitive athletes, hemp seeds are fascinating in many regards. The high magnesium content supports efficient energy production and ensures healthy bones. Abundant vitamin E helps endurance athletes prevent oxidative stress. Containing more high-quality proteins than most other seeds makes hemp seeds an optimal athletes' food.

Since they taste nutty, hulled hemp seeds go nicely with muesli, salads, and many smoothies.

<u>Fact:</u> Hemp seeds are extraordinarily nutritious (containing minerals, vitamins, antioxidants, omega-

3, omega-6, and fiber), and adverse effects are unknown because in some regions of the world (such as China) people have always eaten these seeds. Hemp seeds have a promising future due to their beneficial properties as nutrients and their simple organic cultivation (very robust: no fertilizer or pesticides necessary).

The Real Superfoods

These four superfoods are unmistakably promising, but often quite expensive. If you want to play it safe, focus on the power foods presented in the preceding chapters. Several independent scientific studies have proven the effectiveness of these natural and healthy foods, whether it be beetroot, fenugreek, berries, garlic, flaxseed, turmeric, or dark green leafy vegetables. These foods are easy to integrate into your daily routine and promise astonishing advantages for your next competition.

The Superfood
of the Gladiators

From ancient documents and other historical sources, it is known that gladiators had their own diet, which was adapted to the most extreme challenges in the battle arenas. In the old texts, gladiators are repeatedly called "hordearii," which means "barley eater" or "grain eater" in Latin and was often used as a swear word for gladiators.

Until a few years ago, these were just assumptions from historiography. Today, however, these are scientific facts, as researchers at the Medical University of Vienna were able to verify the special barley diet of gladiators.[1] For this purpose, the scientists examined the bone composition of the fighters in a gladiator cemetery of the 2nd century near the ancient city of Ephesus. At that time, Ephesus was the most important metropolis in the Roman province of Asia. With 200,000 inhabitants, it was also one of the largest cities of the Roman Empire. In such a Roman mega-city, gladiator fights were popular entertainment.

With the help of spectroscopy (a method of analytical

chemistry), stable isotope ratios of elements like carbon, nitrogen, and sulfur were analyzed in the bones of the ancient gladiators. In addition, the researchers measured the ratio of strontium to calcium in the skeletons. This is a significant ratio because high strontium values are definitive evidence of a meat-free diet. To compare the gladiators with the regular population of antiquity, 31 other skeletons of the citizens of Ephesus were examined in addition to the 22 gladiator skeletons.

The scientific analysis of the bone finds revealed the unique diet of the gladiators. Their meals were mainly made up of grains and other plants. Wheat and barley were the basic staple foods, and in some cases, beans were a significant component. Of course, the gladiators also consumed other grains, vegetables, and fruits. Meat and dairy products, as the isotope analysis revealed, were virtually non-existent. From today's perspective, the gladiators were vegans with an unusually high barley consumption.

The performance of gladiators was at least comparable to today's competitive athletes, as only at maximum performance was survival possible in the arena. After all, it was all about life and death. The gladiators got their tremendous energy and stamina from whole-some carbohydrates. Interestingly, the top athletes in endurance sports still use the same highly effective strategy today. Carbo-loading (or carbohydrate loading) is often used to replenish muscle glycogen stores: Before competitions, the athletes consume food abundant in carbohydrates, like whole-wheat pasta. That's why some ambitious athletes call carbo-loading "a pasta party," although of course other carbohydrates, like whole-grain rice or bread, can be just as useful.

The elite fighters of antiquity not only ensured their survival in the battle for life and death with daily carbo-loading but even used special sports drinks. Researchers studying their bones found that the gladiators mixed water with vinegar and vegetable ash, creating one of the first sports drinks in the world. Plant ash also contains electrolytes, such as magnesium or calcium, which are commonly used by athletes for training exposures longer than 60 to 90 minutes.

Unfortunately, this exceptional grain of antiquity, barley, has been entirely ignored by the trendsetters of today's cuisines despite its unique and delicious taste, its versatility, and, last but not least, its numerous health benefits. Many modern superfoods cannot remotely compete with the natural antique barley grain. Fourteen clinical trials in humans from all over the world have clearly shown that barley consumption can effectively reduce not only one but two types of bad cholesterol, thus reducing the risk of heart attacks. Barley consumption can reduce LDL and non-HDL levels by as much as 7%.[2] It contains even more fiber, twice as much protein, and almost half the calories of oats.

Barley contains essential minerals in an optimal bioavailable combination. Potassium, magnesium, and calcium naturally help lower blood pressure. These minerals and others like iron, manganese, and zinc—also contained in barley—contribute to a healthy growth and strengthening of the bones. The ratio of minerals is also important because too much phosphorus with too little calcium can lead to bone loss. Here, barley offers a perfect balance in a natural way, which is not copyable with dietary supplements. Nature, as it does so often, supplies a superior formula in a naturally safe and cost-effective way.

How can you integrate barley into your daily diet? Barley is a real all-rounder in the kitchen. In the morning, you can mix barley flakes in muesli. At noon, barley can be added to risotto instead of rice. In the evening, you can add pearl barley to any vegetable soup. Of course, barley flour can replace ordinary wheat flour in bread and cakes. The slightly nutty flavor brings variety to the diet. The best part: Barley gives you the superpower of the ancient gladiators for today's sports competitions.

*CAESAR'S LEGIONS COMPLAINED
IF THEY GOT TOO MUCH MEAT.
THEY PREFERRED BARLEY AND OTHER GRAINS
WHEN THEY HAD TO FIGHT.[3]*

PRESUMABLY, THE ROMAN SOLDIERS KNEW
THEY COULD ENDURE LONGER WITH PLENTY OF
CARBOHYDRATES.

Scientific Sources of the Chapter Superfoods for Athletes:

1. Stable Isotope and Trace Element Studies on Gladiators and Contemporary Romans from Ephesus (Turkey, 2nd and 3rd Ct. AD) - Implications for Differences in Diet **PLoS ONE** 2014 9(10): e110489, Lösch S, Moghaddam N, Grossschmidt K, Risser DU, Kanz F

2. A systematic review and meta-analysis of randomized controlled trials of the effect of barley β-glucan on LDL-C, non-HDL-C and apoB for cardiovascular disease risk reduction **European Journal of Clinical Nutrition** 2016 Nov;70(11):1239-1245, Ho HV, Sievenpiper JL, Zurbau A, Mejia SB, Jovanovski E, Au-Yeung F, Jenkins AL, Vuksan V

3. History of Civilization, Vol III. Caesar and Christ. Simon and Schuster, New York 1944, Durant, Will

BE
PLANT
VICTORIOUS!

BECOME SUPERHUMANLY STRONG
WITH PLANT-BASED FOODS!

*NOBODY WHO EVER GAVE
HIS BEST REGRETTED IT.*

GEORGE HALAS

Made in the USA
San Bernardino, CA
24 September 2018